JOU.

OF A WOMAN

A poetic ensemble ...

Out From Pain

Poetry & Prose By

**Willetta J. Davis, Valencia V. Gibson, Jeslyn Lewis,
Elisha McCardell, J.M. Perkins, Kimberly Monique Smith
and Alisha Williams**

**

ISBN: 9781089542490 (paperback)

Front cover image by Unknown Artist
Book design by Willetta J. Davis

Printed by Kindle Publishing, Inc., in the United States of America.

First printing, 2019.

LettesReadBooks Publishing
Shreveport, LA

DEDICATION

This book is dedicated to the fighters, survivors and loved ones lost to breast cancer, domestic violence and mental illness.

To Beauty who does not know that she is Beautiful

To Victory who does not know that she is Victorious

ACKNOWLEDGEMENTS

To God be the Glory, because without Him none of this would have been possible. He gave me this gift - this vision of Journey of a Woman. He spoke to me and I listened. I am so wonderfully grateful for this journey and more so elated for the beloved visionaries who accepted to take this journey, also. To the lovely ladies with a vision and a purpose: Valencia, Jeslyn, Elisha, Jont'e, Kimberly and Alisha. Thank you for taking this journey. You are AWESOME! I am forever grateful for my "Inspirational" Brother and Sister, poet and poetess: Roosevelt Wright and Pascha Gibson, who inspired me to find my inner voice and not be afraid to express my deep most inner feelings. To Poetic X, thank you for the realization that an "old" piece is a "new" piece to a new audience. To Team Davis 9, my husband and children (my Jewels) thank you for believing and supporting me. Thank you for giving me my "Me-Time and Mommy Time" in order to complete this vision. Foremost, I would like to thank my "Circle" (extended family and friends), you know who you are. Thank you for never doubting and discouraging me (privately or personally) to focus on anything else, but what I was set out to do. Thank you for always believing in my gift and for cheering and encouraging me from the sideline. Forever be blessed and always be inspired! **-Willetta J. Davis**

To my Grandmother Margie N. Adams who always believed in my abilities to succeed and beat the odds. To my parents who were young and trying to figure this parenting thing out. To my aunt who taught me the facts of life and inspired me to never give up on my goals. To my husband and life partner who supports any and every endeavor, to my children who want so badly for their mother to be the greatest mom who ever lived. And most important, God who takes priority over all, her ultimate motivation, creator, and originator of all of the gifts and talents she possesses. **-Valencia Gibson**

To the one who flies for me when my wings are bruised and flies with me as I soar, my mother, Dorothy Hawkins Lewis; to my mentor and God-mother, Bernadine Haley Davenport; and to three women of the Hawkins Clan that I know have my back, Janie W. McKenzie, Myra McKenzie-Harris and JoLynette H. Crayton. On my journey to womanhood the 5 of you have impacted my life in ways you can never imagine. Merely saying thank you is not sufficient. I am forever indebted to you. Such big shoes to fill...To my beautiful diamonds in the mirror, Paydrea D. Lewis, Pavia D. Brown and Talisa L. Brown, on your journey to becoming women, you will make some missteps, but if you remember to lean NOT to your own understanding, be still and KNOW that God is God and patiently wait to see the salvation of the Lord, you shall reap the rewards stored up with your names on them. Finally, to my sisters (there are too many of you to name) ... my love and gratitude to you goes without saying.

-Jeslyn Lewis

To my mom Gloria Jean Wiley and grandmother, Beulah Wiley. Thank you. You are forever loved. **-Kimberly Monique Smith**

I would like to dedicate this book and give thanks to my wonderful and lovely children, CJ, Krischan, AJ and Gabby. Mommy loves you all. **-Elisha McCardell**

I would like to enter His gates with thanksgiving and praise. Thank my heavenly Father for blessing me with a gift and talent that I still have trouble in believing at times. But, Lord you knew me and you knew my inadequacy. But, by Your grace I am enough. You remind me that my gifts and talents will make room for me, only if I believe. Thank You for pouring into me so I can pour out to others. I would love to acknowledge my great Aunt Eula, who gave me wisdom when I didn't want to heed or hear it. I want to say thank you to my mother whom is with me daily in spirit. They don't make them like you anymore. I can only instill in my kids and other young ladies what you have instilled in me. I would like to thank my children for life lessons as a parent and stamping great moment and memories in spirit. Giving this life a new fragrance and definition of what it means to live and count it all joy. To my husband that dives deep into my intellect to help usher out the greatest parts of me that I have yet to discover. Thank you for understanding me and allowing me to be authentically me. To my Aunt Denise, you see in me what I don't see, you pull out the best in me. Thank you for sharing memories of my mother with me. Thank you for loving me and stepping up when she passed. Thank you for your love, kindness and patience. To my Sister Camesha, thank you for being my little big sister and encouraging me, through encouraging you. You are special to me, I love you. To those that read this, know that you are great and no matter what you think of yourself, your gifts and talents will make room for you. Don't allow what others are doing to take your focus from your own purpose and destiny. **-J. M. Perkins**

I would like to eternally thank God for His grace, mercy, gifts, and opportunities. I would like to thank you Willetta Davis, a million times over for the opportunity to contribute to your Manuscript Compilation. You are such an Angel, Powerful Poet, and Dynamic Woman of God. I would also, like to thank Poetic X for his poetic ambition, expression, leadership and drive. I would also like to thank ArtistSwagg, Yahoo groups, The Poetry Corner and The Poetry Spot. God bless you and your platforms. Long live poetry. **-Alisha Williams**

CONTENTS

CHAPTER THREE

CHAPTER FOUR

CHAPTER FIVE

CHAPTER SIX

CHAPTER SEVEN

CHAPTER EIGHT

Introduction

As we stand on the shoulders of Queen Mother Maya, Sistah Nikki, Lady Michelle and many others, we are elated to share *Journey of a Woman*. We as women, like earth, wind, fire and water are essential to life! On our journeys we are faced with obstacles that drop like boulders. We have to stand together to contribute to the evisceration of being unloved, abused, ill-treated, taken for granted, overlooked, misunderstood and disrespected. This book will share age old wisdom, unprecedented knowledge and immeasurable love. It was developed to educate, enrich, validate, enlighten, intrigue, empower as well as entertain. This journey through spoken word was birthed by women who have loved, lost, redesigned, started over and holistically recharged. It is fundamental to life's library. Lose yourself in the extreme self-care this collection of treasure offers. Prepare to be ushered into another dimension through this *Journey of a Woman*.

-Jeslyn Lewis

For Mama & Stephanie
(My Angels)

Chapter One

DESTINY'S END

Elisha McCardell
Dear God

I thank you for carrying me over obstacles larger than the expanse from the heaven and earth.

I thank you for creating beliefs within me that has sustained me during times I felt lower than the valleys that crisscrossed throughout the world.

I thank you for opening doors far larger than the oceans are wide.

You are a Father that doesn't forget.

You are a Father who does what it takes to create assurance within your children.

You are my Father, Amen.

Willetta J. Davis

Journey

If you knew my journey would you still judge me? Or would you understand that my right now is not where I use to be? If you knew my journey.

I made some wrong decisions when I started out on this road. I didn't have no direction I didn't know which way to go. Should I go left? Should I go right? Reverse or move on? I'm stuck at my crossroads of life facing every obstacle.

If you knew my journey.

I've been on the run half my life- spinning out of control. I made some wrong turns on one- ways, going down wrong ways, and closed roads. I've been hit and run over, side swiped and run off roads. I was stranded in HELL hot deserts- even my mirages had me paying tolls.

If you knew my journey.

This journey hasn't been easy- it's definitely been a trip! I've been broken down, flattened, rear-ended, whiplashed and whipped. I turned on the radio hoping to hear my favorite song. ***Highway to Hell*** * was all that played every day- all day long! I'm out of control wondering ***What's Going On***? *

I'm seeing signs of
MAYHEM
But ...
YOU'RE IN GOOD HANDS*
Keep moving on because...

G od's

P rotective

S ervice...won't steer you wrong!

If you knew my journey

I had to make a trade-in on some new friends. Because, my old friends were like lemons- stuck… nowhere to go… battery dead… pulled over… ticketed… tagged… towed off roads; always taking the HIGH road but always come down feeling low- drinking and driving…driving drunk. Death riding in the trunk. I was **D**one **W**ith **I**gnorance. It was time to go!

I jumped out and let them roll on. No more playing red light, green light…STOP! That part of me is gone. No turning back… just praying they don't crash and burn… hoping one day soon they will learn. Life is not an easy street but, **G**od's **A**lmighty **S**ervice saved me.

If you knew my journey

I wondered on this road a long time ago…wondering, why I am not dead after all I've been through. What I found out…what I probably already knew…and now I know. I was covered ALL this time with **Assurance Insurance** *"It follows you EVERYWHERE you go."*

Valencia V. Gibson

OVERCOMER

Obstacles helped me discover the faith I needed to leap over the hurdles that were in my way.

Victory came after the struggles, and the power of God stepped in to save the day.

Everlasting love covered my past.

Redemption changed my life.

Commitment is what I'm giving to stay focused as a daughter, mother and wife.

Opportunities are in my favor, and I've learned to go wherever I'm led.

Making the best of this life, no matter what, I'm embracing the journey up ahead.

Echoing words of encouragement over my life daily. Even though things aren't always what they seem.

Revelation is what I am most grateful for, I am confident I can overcome anything.

Alisha Williams
Attention

People don't get me
So what,
It's like I'm wired weird
I imagine myself in my own head
Telling you, I want my son Evette.
Nobody gets it
But I do
I love that girl in the mirror
With a bruise right there
But it's healing
Soon, you won't be able to see it.
Let this pen be my therapy
Spill my emotions onto these pages
Until they are dripping with the iodine soaked tears I cried in
private
Then, pat myself on the back
And say get up and get back out there
You ain't special
Everybody got a story to tell
Lift up your brothers and sisters
Every chance you get
That is how you grow
Think about others before
you think about self

Jeslyn Lewis

Iridescent Portraits
Inspired by Myra L. McKenzie & Kofi N. Hensley-Hawkins

I've found that in life we encounter the ugly, the good, and
unfortunately the bad;
Sometimes we are happy, yet inevitably sometimes we are
sad~
Love comes and may even stay or without warning love
goes:
Will life's lemons come with sugar? That nobody knows~
But we have to focus on how to find the lining behind every
dark cloud;
At times silence is required, yet other times you must speak
ALOUD!
Can you say...portraits of iridescence?

It may be your time right now, but sooner or later mine will
come as well;
You may be floating on angel wings today, but tomorrow
may be a living hell~
You have to watch what you say to folks, 'cause you reap
what you sow you know;
And stop being so judgmental, the bad seeds you plant will
surely grow.

Life has a funny way of keeping us all in line;
Everyday He gives us new mercy, but you never know, this
may be your last time~
Let's refer to it as, let's see, iridescent portraits...

Yellow may be your color today; tomorrow may be blue or
green;
It's important that you mean what you say and only say
what you really mean!
Never form an opinion of a book only by the cover;

What you thought was yours forever could soon be replaced
by another~
Keep your eyes on the ultimate prize; pray about every
choice;
Old wives' fables are like sounding brass, no need for that
excess noise~
Just an illusion known as portraits of iridescence...

Things ain't always what they seem and every smile ain't for
real;
Stay true yourself always, stay in touch with how you really
feel~
Toss away all wooden nickels by avoiding negative folk;
Keep Christ first in your life and upon you surely to take his
yoke!
Life won't be a crystal stairway so careful how you move
your feet;
Healing comes from exposing secrets, but you should still be
cautiously discreet.
I'll say it again, iridescent portraits.

Use every stepping stone thrown on your path as an
elevator to the next level;
And remember what your elders say, for every level
awaiting is a new devil!
Let nothing hinder your progress, always take life by the
horns;
God has a special task for every child that is of a woman
born~
For every twist and turn in life, God has an ultimate plan;
Things will never be the same from day to day,
but no matter what the problem just remember through
Christ,

YOU CAN!!!
It's just that each portrait of you is...iridescent~

Willetta J. Davis

#blessed

my life is a mess
i'm undressed
naked to the world!
lost and confused-
abused and bruised
Amazing Grace
please save this little brown girl
all hope is gone
abandoned-
stranded-
all alone
nowhere or no one to turn to
branded -
once a whole soul
now a hole in me-
burned through!
a wretch-
so far fetched
i don't know what to do
i believe all false
and damn all truths
my greatest pleasure
is being lied to
i was too blind to see
who and what was
in front of me
a fool too foolishly
foolish
to follow the footsteps in front
of me
that would lead me
where i'm supposed to be
when i'm supposed to be
-

how sweet the sound
Amazing Grace
thank You for saving
this little brown
turning me around
placing me on the
righteous path
picking me up
when I was down
making
mending
molding me
whole again
giving my life
a new meaning-

a new #
thank You for
cleansing me
filling my cup
until it runneth over
i don't believe in luck-
it's unlucky
i believe in His powers
shower me with
Your **#blessing**
giving me a new dressing on this journey

Valencia V. Gibson
Latter Days

They didn't see you, when you
Prayed all night in your loneliness
Cried all night in your rejection
Starved all night in your lack
Was in bondage in your mental prison
Contemplated thoughts of giving up in your valley

Oh, no they thought it came easy... Especially when they didn't see you being:
Stretched out of your comfort zone
Forced to get over those who rejected you
Challenged to trust in God's provision alone
Empowered to choose freedom
Pushed to reach your mountain top no matter how you felt

Which is why your:

Relationship with God is unmatched
Chains have been broken
Joy can no longer be stolen
Heart is no longer fragile
Confidence is no longer shaken
Faith is no longer unstable
Love walk is so strong
Spirit rejects guilt, and shame
Cycles are broken in Jesus Name
Generational curses are shattered, and are being returned to the sender
Yes, you now know what it means to speak, offer, come and go in perfect peace
Because you stopped holding on to your life, accepted the life Jesus Christ set before you, and now when you say you have too much to lose you really mean it, and truly believe it
    Be Blessed and Good Night Family

J.M. Perkins
Wash Your Face

Never lose your identity in someone else's mental setback.

Sometimes as women we lose ourselves in building men. I call this "building bears."

You have allowed time to slip away and all of your hopes and dreams are bottled up in a jar like preserves and set aside and labeled, "for emergencies only."

You massage heads, stroke egos, encourage dry bones and whisper revelations in the ear of the potential laying next to you as he sleeps in hopes that when he awakes, he is motivated and inspired to take over the world. You have given him gas to believe that he is more than a conqueror.

You oil his feet with your prayers from your alabaster box.

You put him first, always and foremost, but what about you.

You walk around the house in your favorite robe, hair scarf and oversized socks, meeting all the needs of everyone around you. You are their super woman. But to you there is nothing super or grand about you. You are doing what you should because for a moment if you didn't, it wouldn't get done, at least not the way you do it.

You finally look at yourself in the mirror. Not like any other day. I mean you look at yourself every day. You look at yourself when you brush your teeth, do your hair, wash your face and even size your own self up when you put on your clothes. You even point out your attributes and dislikes about yourself.

But this day you take a good look and realize your face hasn't been washed at all.

Think about how you feel when you wash off the makeup and concealer and you look at yourself, not the self that you pretend to be, but you.

When you wash your face after a cry that you cried from your soul, snot and all. You take the towel as hot as you can take it and rub it across your face as if you are washing all your sorrows away. You look in the mirror and see yourself!

Washed face, eyes wide open. You see yourself clearly. You take the jar of preserves filled with your hope and dreams marked, "for emergencies only," blow the dust off and open it.

As you open the jar something in you jumps. Your spirit has awakened as you have breathed the breath of life back into your purpose. By washing your face, you realized you can live out the dreams you hoped for.

No more gleaning behind for someone's leftovers because God has something set aside just for you.

So, you wash your face, anoint yourself and put on your cape and become the woman that God has created you to be-

Ruth, go after your dreams and live them out loud!

Chapter Two

Cracked Not Broken

J.M. Perkins
Winter of My Soul

Fall is here which happens to be my favorite time of year. The leaves fall gracefully to the ground as the ground smiles with colorful thoughts of mercy. Winter prepares itself for its next journey as it exposes the truth of my trust in God. Its dawn, our meeting time; the time I take out and indulge in your presence, back in your love as I take out communion with my Father, the lover of my soul. Dew accompanies the wind, as it slowly takes place and makes a quilt on the pasture. I realize, it's time to address the issues in the basement of my being that cries out in the silent night which no one hears but You. You have been ready to listen, but I haven't been submissive to talk. I'm ready as icicles roll down my rosemary cheeks flushed with anxiety.

As a young girl I yearned the love and attention from my earthen father. He expressed his love with used and worn gifts and replaced his time with pocket change. I couldn't understand how a foreign estranged woman could come into our world and change the momentum of our relationship. This was a woman whom never expressed unconditional love for me, a woman that often treated me like I was an infidel child. When the truth of the matter is, I was here first. My life was invaded, and a void grew with deep roots from childhood to adulthood. As I get down to the matter of the winter of my soul, stainless tears continue to soar down my face. He wipes them away with His napkin of compassion and grace as I continue to express my need for Him. All I wanted was for him to love me, speak up for me, and spend time with me with no excuses. Every excuse was my fault. Even as a child it was my fault for not being in pictures or involved in trips. She consistently, silently and deliberately competed her daughter with me as jealously became evident. I questioned, "How can an adult be jealous and have so much hate against an innocent child? Why me? Vengeance is the Lords as her actions toward me became her own curse with her own family. As I watch from a long handled spoon as this generational curse attacks my son and now involves her grandson, my heart explodes as my son noticed what I once did at his age. His eyes take on the look of my eyes as a forgotten child. He is now in the position as I was, treated like the black sheep with a front porch relationship. I reflect on my relationship with my Father in heaven. I longed for a love I've always had. It was because of You I live, have life and experience life more abundantly. You broke my heart with my father just to mend it in You. You nurtured me to be a giver and love those that rightfully hurt me from birth. I possess an anointing as an intercessor, evangelist, peacemaker and healer to those around me. When I had nowhere to stay, I found refuge in You. With no food to eat, I ate your word as it filled me and gave me a new appetite. I quickly realized in my wilderness that I can only depend on You, which deepened my love and trust for You. Doors slammed in my face and loved ones turned their backs on me and made excuses, but You were there. You loved me through my childhood when it tried to break me. You rescued me from my past and as this curse breaks and season pass; Your love is a shelter for me that will eternally last.

Valencia V. Gibson

If I could see you today, what might I'd say...

Dear rapist,

When you touched me, I had no clue that what you did...
Would leave a scar so very deep, that I would cringe when my
husband caressed me, and fear for the safety of my kids.

Dear abuser,

You were so kind in the beginning, the connection we shared
was unmatched. I told myself I had goals of my own, so I tried not
to get too attached.

Who knew that one day in a conversation that my loyalty to
my dreams and my love for you would compete for first place?

I lost myself at the impact of your hand across the most
sensitive parts of my face.

We scuffled, and you choked me, then carried me to the edge
of the stairs, if it wasn't for your brother... I think to myself, as I re-
live those nightmares.

Never trusting the one who's never lifted a finger, thinking
one day he could change too. Then I snap out of it once I am
reminded, that he is nowhere close to you!

Dear Dealer,

I was fourteen, I know I should have stayed in a child's
place, but I needed something to relax my mind, and every now and
then put a pep in my pace.

You knew better, so why did you entertain me? For the
money, yea I know. It was hard. I'm not blaming you for my actions,
but the night I almost died from that overdose though...

Dear Cheater,

I felt the difference in the strokes you delivered to me. The way that you finished so quickly in the midst of our intimacy.

The way that you criticized my looks, my size, and how I never listened to you.

The fact that you tried to justify and blame me for the actions you chose, for a temporary moment of gratification, you traded it all for these... I forgave you...

Dear Adults,

Who were responsible for my upbringing, how could you have known. That in a minute of passion, a child would be born before you would become fully grown.

That I would grow up full of ambition to forgive, love, and make peace. To never hold you captive in the prison of my heart for the things that happened to me.

It was rough no doubt; many roads I did trod. But I'm casting my shame into the sea as I go and giving my past hurts over to God.

If I could see you today... I forgive you, is what I would say...

Willetta J. Davis

EXPRESSIONS

I loved him in an odd way; until the day his hands went across my face. Though, he built his love for me on lies, I still loved him with no regrets. Yet, shocked into disbelief that those hands would ever touch me so violently. When before, they would caress and sensationalize my intimacy.

I shake away the foolish thoughts that were now coming over me. Realizing his new expression of "love", hunted by the expression "love hurts"- definitely not this way, I know!

I moved my eyes slowly across his hardened lips, as his voice violated the virgin day. Though his voice rolled like thunder, I could only see the lightning in his eyes. I could not hear anything but, the ringing in my ears and that small voice saying "leave".

Once again, I'm drowning in his words: "I LOVE YOU", "I'LL NEVER HURT YOU".

Damn my face hurts. Damn my body hurts. DAMN YOU!! Damn this pain...damn the emotional ability of loving you. Damn these tears that want to fall from my burning eyes...stream across my broken nose... anchor from my busted lips... fall into my bloody mouth- to taste its saltiness. Damn those run-away tears that want to cover my chin and broken neck and blanket my bruised breasts. DAMN YOU!!

I continue to fight the hurt, the pain, the tears. I DARE to even THINK about "ALL THESE YEARS!" I DARE to THINK about the ALWAYS AND FOREVERS*, LET'S STAY TOGETHERS*, MAKE IT LAST FOREVERS*, FAKE KISSES, IMITATION HUGS, NOT SO WELL WISHES AND MAKE -BELIEVE LOVE!

I dare to let him see my weakness. I dare to let him know how I feel. I dare to let him know how much I truly loved him. Because...now I know how much he truly LOVED me.

Elisha McCardell

Strong Woman

I remember when he called me strong. It was the day after I had forgiven him for cheating on me.

"No other woman is like you! You are a STRONG WOMAN!"

I remember when he called me strong. It was when I was able to get us out of the bind because he spent all of our bill money.

"I am so lucky to have you. You are amazingly a STRONG WOMAN."

It took me a while to realize that this badge of strength was really an excuse for him to do with me as he pleased. The belief is that strong women are able to get through any obstacle. I explained to him that I was not strong, and his perspective is only a result of him being so weak.

Kimberly Monique Smith

The Push

He pushed me against the wall that made my head spin around and around again. Instead of seeing stars, I saw balloons floating in front of me that protected me from his blows. Numbness overshadowed me as a cloud does the sun. I tried to move but all I could do was stand against the wall.

I heard a roar as he came again with greater force alarming me this time I would fall for sure. My skin; my beautiful black skin was glued to the wall awaiting the pain to break me up. Suddenly those balloons floated in front of me soft as a cotton ball cloud and cushioned the blows.

He became angrier punching only the balloons and hitting nothing but the air. He stumbled and the balloons scattered; he fell against the wall and slithered down. I pushed myself from the wall and stepped right over him. As I walked away, I looked back at that wall realizing it saved my life from the push that spanned my head around and around again.

I vowed to myself I would never allow another push of the hand throw me into a wall.

Valencia V. Gibson

Accountable for My Heart

I saw my heart sitting on the edge of the bed, comfortably resting on the sheets of some cheap motel.

I can remember it like it was yesterday.

The soap, the perfume, the smell of Newport cigarettes and Brandy, glasses half empty, mouths printed on the rims.

Yes, I remember the moment I climbed through the window of his soul and reigned on her contentment.

That contentment a person has, when they think no one knows their doings, their dealings, their iniquitous feelings.

Oh! I was loud too, messy, ill prepared, and reckless. Not concerned about the aftermath of crashing the masquerade I had stumbled upon.

I said to myself love will make you do some insane, out of your mind, I got time, to run out here in the middle of the night crazy A** things. Does it really?

Is it really love that made me go, or is it the allowance I gave my heart to hurt me?

Is it the portion of my heart I allowed him to spend, when I became one with a low down, lying, cheating, drinking, manipulating, smooth talking, dimple bearing (whew)...? I digress...

The point is... I saw my heart in the hands of a napper a long time ago, and I didn't try to save, I gave, it away willingly.

So, he took it... He had the nerve to sit our heart at the edge of that bed, in comfort and rest it upon those sheets of that cheap motel.

Yea, that pain. I recall it as if it was the very moment, I knocked on that door. That moment he didn't answer the call of love anymore.

That moment I heard his movement and climbed through the window of his soul. I ripped that weighted blanket of security, she was so peacefully nestled in right off of her.

I reigned on her contentment, the kind she felt as if I'd never find out, I knew it was her all along...

Wreaking of the smell of bar soap, distasteful perfume, smoke on her lips and the taste of his brandy cologne...

Kimberly Monique Smith
True Grit

Tonight is cold and quiet like my heart was months ago. Cold from the hurt that lived within me; cold and hard like the ground I walked. I wondered if my heart would ever feel free as it once did. Once upon a time, my heart was warm, cozy, and eager for the next laugh. I cannot remember when it stopped feeling that way; it happened so suddenly. How strange one encounter can change your life and the way you perceive things. How people can literally torment you without ever speaking to you. How odd when you allow them to control every inch of your life just by their sight. How your heart turns from warm and cozy to cold and uncertain. How driving home on a Friday night makes you feel as if you going to a forbidden place where no one wants you. How staying in on Saturdays because of what you see will cause a knot in your stomach so tight you become nauseous. Feeling anxiety attacks on Wednesdays when you wake knowing later in the evening you will have to face reality at 6. Migraines, sleepiness nights, Ambien, Lortab, vodka all that poison that made you their addict. Allowing people to take possession of your actions, your joy, your sight, every feeling within your being that leaves you naked in public. Feeling their laughs and hearing their whispers of you. Maybe they did not laugh but my heart said hell yeah they are mocking me. Struggling to break free from all those insane thoughts you felt. Wishing you were the woman, you once were before that Saturday night. Screaming obscene gestures to yourself because there's no one to neither listen nor care. Wishing it was them you were screaming those gestures too. Despising them yes, I finally said it; feeling free once, it evicted from my lips and heart, breathing insanely after confessing my true feelings. Praying silently to God, please forgive me for feeling those emotions. At this moment, I exhale sanely through my words. My heart suddenly feels warm and cozy as if I am sitting in front of the fireplace sipping on a glass of red wine with my notebook and a blue pen by my side, wearing pink flannel jammies and fuzzy socks with my hair up in a ponytail. Smiling like a silly person but surely a sane one. A bowl of popcorn in my lap, legs crossed on a leather sofa. My heart is Happy; happy that craziness was over, gone kaput. Poison that almost destroyed me months ago but became the medicine I needed to taste the sweet honeysuckle in the morning dew. Tonight is warm and cozy just like my heart.

Elisha McCardell

She Could Not Be Saved

I looked into the distance searching for the lifeliness that I embodied for many.

Where was the white stallion and the prince to race me across the finish line?

A black hole that refused to give life or light, I existed.

The solitude was the result of those who came and left.

A used paper to clear away excrement.

No longer needed.

The sacrificial lamb that others feasted on.

I was the emptied lover of leeches.

The cries for help became whispers through the sounds of the hurricane.

Regardless of the storms they expected me to survive.

The last soldier on the battlefield.

The captain on a sinking ship.

My tears fell like leaves near the gutter.

Swept into a place no one knew existed.

I surrendered myself to life and refused hope.

I flew my white flag.

I drifted into the abyss waiting for the tide

take carry me to a place where no one else breathed.

Kimberly Monique Smith

Essence of Love

That sweet aching undying love I had for you

that dwelled in the depth of my heart,

in the socket of my eyes,

on the edge of my fingers,

on the swirl of my tongue

every time I uttered your name;

that causes an arch in my back whenever I thought of you,

was wasted;

it was never intended to be, well at least not with you.

I happily realized it was never meant to reach any potential between us.

This LOVE I'm rapping about was for ME and only ME.

To mend my wayward heart, to give my eyes a new perspective;

on how love should truly be received from one to another.

To taste the intoxicating dew on the tips of my fingers and a reviving swirl to my tongue.

My LOVE gave me the essence to know when to keep my back straight and how to wait on the TRUE arch man.

It's funny, you probably think I'm rattled because my LOVE for YOU failed, but I'm not;

because baby I realized YOU never could have handled it anyway.

So, I thank YOU for being who YOU were to ME

because I never would have known the Essence of true LOVE

Alisha Williams

Love Was or Love Is

What happens on that day when I no longer see love in your face
When your eyes don't call me
And my mind stop replaying the same soap box episode where you asked me to trust you
And I threw my mind and emotions to the wind and daydreamed of every way we would love each other
Forever it was
Until reality hit
And took my love away with it
Every beat grew faint
Felt it breaking
Like a deafened pulse that I searched
For frantically and flat lined
Revive the love that was in me
Resuscitate the longings of my romanticism
With one rose in a vase
Left on the doorstop of my heart
Pulling the petals of a sweetened rose
He loves me
He loves me not
Stop playing with my heart
And let me go
So the husband that's meant to say
I do to me can come forth
if it's not you
Cool?
Because my preverbal clock is ticking
And I don't want to drown in a pool of shallow water
Grasping for trinkets of your time
Rewind, I'm a woman
No, better yet I'm a wife
And I'm going to show that
To the husband to be
He will cherish me

Be the yin to my yang
Breathing easy
Co-existing
Floating in
Between the honeymoon stage
Love pays the balance
When you treat her right
Alright

Jeslyn Lewis

Love Is A Battlefield*

Love is a Battlefield, yep that's just how I see it
The thought of being in love makes me feel like a warrior,
always on the defensive,
protecting my heart so I don't get caught up in the bull shit
of it.
Bobbin' and weaving my way through the thick of it
Sticking and moving causing a little resentment
But at the end of the day, I'm looking out for number 1 and that's just me;
Love has yet to discover my name and until it does,
I'll smile a little here;
Flirt a little there,
until my one comes along
the one who can tell me something I don't already know
Or take me places I haven't been;
realize it's about a soul connection as well as about being best friends
The love I've known so far has been tainted with lies,
deception, and a whole lot of other bull shit
Oh excuse me for sounding like the mad black woman,
I just believe in calling shit like I see it... keeping it 100 and always being legit.
I guess I was in love with the idea of being in love huh?
Stumbling in the dark looking in all the wrong faces
Ending up lonely and in desperate places
But that was back then, because now,
shiddd it's all about me
Looking great and feeling good,
damn being on that battlefield
And...
Giving him something he can feel
He better let ME know HIS love is real
Cause ain't nobody got time fa allat,
"Where you going baby," "who is that ma?"

"Why you got on make-up bae," "why you gotta wear yo jeans so tight boo?"
Miss me with all that bull shit, you better be worried about who's foolin' who?
Cause what you see ain't always what you get
And trust me, you ain't seen JesLovely yet
I love hard, and don't miss a beat
But until it's someone worthy of my heart;
Spiritual, established, adventurous, and smart
I'll be cruising to the beat of my own drum
Having fun, taking life as it comes
No I'm not an angry black woman;
I'm a black woman who has channeled her anger into loving herself fiercely!
Seeing and acknowledging that I'm a no-nonsense, zero tolerance for bullshit,
Beautiful, intelligent, gifted black queen who is worth the war
Down for the cause, and while I may have a few scars
The man that's FOR me will see those scars and honor them
Worship them and be the caregiver thereof
That's when I'll know he's my one and only love
He'll seek to never reopen those wounds or add to them
He'll know that I don't seek to fulfill myself with him,
because I'm too full of me
And it's cool if you disagree…
But it'll be his charge to get inside my heart and make himself at home
He'll look at me and say Beautiful…Good morning
It will be a good morning because he awakened next to this queen.
He'll probably not even realize he's awake, looking at this dream
Me, the one who won't take his kindness for weakness
But also the one who will not forsake my own happiness
No, what I will do is wait for my king
To enter my queendom,
accept his majestic seat on the throne
And make me his very own
I will not settle for fly by nighters

who are only there for a night
Looking for a flight......... aboard my love jet
Riding my waves of ecstasy
So he can be a 24-hour legacy
Helllllll nawh
He better go and come again
We ain't even them kinda friends
The only benefit he'll get
is to be in my presence
Pledge his allegiance
To me
Ms. JesLovely
A beautiful butterfly flapping her pretty wings
Stirring and shaking up some things
Letting em know
That to be with me, he gots to be A-one
Because queens don't step down off their thrones
They wait for the warrior to get off the battlefield
Prove that he is the real deal
Put down his sword, and pry the sword from my hand
This takes a seasoned man
He must tear down the walls I've built around my heart
Chase away past fears, and make a brand new start
See I'm not an angry black woman, mad about a failed relationship
I'm a beautiful black queen who is done with lies and bull shit!
Because real eyes realize real lies and KNOW that
Love, Love is a battlefield but sometimes, it is worth it.

J. M. Perkins

The Exam

I bit the fruit and was deceived as the snake whispered in my ear. Pleasing to the eyes, but deadly for the spirit and soul. I thought he was the ONE! He smelled like him, dressed like him, walked like him and talked like him. He even praised and prayed like him. He had a potential and plan. He displayed strong, independent, confidence with godly characteristics. As the veil lifted from my face and eyes, I saw the warning signs but didn't heed them. I was addicted to the possibility of what could be, not the truth that was standing in front of me. He was unfaithful, immature and discontent. His words didn't match up with his actions. His actions spoke louder, and they were perverted. He was confused and easily influenced by others visions and dreams as he tried to produce and structure them as his own. He was easily deceived by estranged woman with the ambition and character traits of Jezebel and Delilah. He was motivated by the approval of others as he pursued the wide way. His words were slick as honey, captivating with every word. He was a womanizer at heart. He was damaged goods who was not pruned, healed or established by God. He was blessing himself and quoted that God did it. Confident in his looks rather than how God looked at Him. He used the word of God to fit his situation instead of allowing the word to cleanse his way or mold his heart. He loved me in his own way but not like Christ loves the church. His love was abusive and full of empty promises. Love, a word of action. A restraining word that had me bound in bondage longer than my season. I was like the Israelites who stayed longer than they should have. I was disobedient and risking my chances of getting to the promise land as God promised. My encounter was meant to be a season, but I insisted on a lifetime. God cut the chains and broke the yoke and I was free. He commands me, "Not to be entangled again with a yoke of bondage. I shared all my visions, dreams and hopes for the future with a person who was only meant for a temporal moment. God redeemed and restored me, He gave me new visions, dreams, ambitions, desires and talents; which are only molded and made for me. They will only persevere and manifest through me. I bought sense with a high price and learned quickly. They that wait on the Lord shall renew their strength and lessen the chance of disaster and destruction. Warnings are always present, and you will know the tree by the fruit it bears.

Don't bite the fruit- EVE, examine it first!

Chapter Three

Remembering You

Willetta J. Davis
The Measure of Moments
For Tonia

Time waits for no one
And, time is a delicate and precious thing
Every second, every minute, every hour, creates moments
that become memories
The measure of moments is about what you do
It's about what you say
It's about how you live...how you give
How you embrace the day
It is in those moments that take your breath away
The measure of moments is how we treat each other
How we make each other feel
It is the measure of moments that feels surreal.

The measure of moments...

It's like the first breath of a baby-
the first gaze into its Mother's eyes
It's like the excitement you feel when you're surprised
It's like the influences of things that create emotions
It's like cascades that falls into river spring's that kisses the
mouths of lakes, seas & oceans

The measure of moments...

It's like the flight of an eagle as it soars high
It's like the formation of clouds that passes us by
It's like the day of a new dawn and how the morning speaks
to you
It's like the stars in the night sky and how we are kissed by
the moon
The measure of moments is God's everlasting love He has for
me and you
Let's take this moment to cherish the love as Loved one's do

In making every minute count now until eternity
Creating moments of...

Love, Peace, Joy and Harmony

Because...
The measure of this moment are the sweet memories created
by you and me

J. M. Perkins
A Daughters' Sorrow

Overwhelmed with the remembrance of you as tears stampeded down my face. I embrace thoughts of your tender hugs, kisses and daily encouragement. My life with you was easy, peaceful, calm and full. The scent of you has never faded away from my senses -the scent of fresh cotton and roses. I have always been captivated by the essence of your beauty. I developed a real definition of a virtuous woman, a nurturer, a secret keeper with a quiet spirit housed within a mother. You tried your best not to spoil us or spare the rod. You trained us up the way we should go and now we are older it has not fallen far from us. You would be proud. You were a woman after God's own heart. You petitioned Him daily for guidance for your own life. You stayed in the face of God, as I found letters, notes and scriptures written out by your craftsmanship exposing your love and need for Him. The more you sought Him, the more you taught us. The more you prayed to Him, the more you prayed and covered us. The more He provided for you, the more you gave us. You were a giver, a cheerful giver with a generous heart and spirit. I witnessed you sacrifice your last so we could have. You didn't eat until we were fulfilled. You loved unconditionally with full capacity. You displayed agape, hospitality and clothed with strength. You walked on water and showed no fear for the future, even at your darkest moment. You always had a plan and worked it. You never complained in times of struggle, but you endured it and by His grace, you overcame it. You were soft spoken but owned every word spoken. A woman of great integrity with noble and loyal character. You taught me to pray. I searched for you in others but soon realized the spirit of you only resides in me, for you are with me. You are forever an angel in my heart, whose presence is graced in heaven.

Valencia V. Gibson
A Mother, Daughter Connection

Mom I had a dream that I woke up from a long rest.
I placed my feet on the ground, and I heard your voice in my head...
You said baby girl this life consists of many tests. So, march!
Baby march to the beat of your own drum.
You can stop and smell the roses, but don't twiddle your thumbs.
I replied I hear the beating sound, but of the direction I am unsure.
I'll keep walking one foot in front of the other, and off the path I dare not stray.
Whether curved, with many twists and turns, narrow or straight. You said march anyway. Mom I heard your voice say...
You can't settle for less, not after the pain I've endured.
Two minutes of pleasure, fourteen hours of labor, and a broken heart that still hasn't been cured.
I don't want you picking of pieces behind someone, some thing, from your past.
Keep marching baby, keep marching, you'll be there in no time.
Mom I had a dream, I heard your voice clearly in my mind.
Now I'm convinced I've found the sound,
that will lead me to the way,
I just thought I'd share this dream with
you before I start my day.
Love you mom!

Willetta J. Davis
Touching Memories

Years have passed since I've touched these walls
Breathe in yesterday's perfume that lingered
Stared at open spaces where I once played

I close my eyes to remember those faded memories

So, I embrace the love left that comforted my soul
It's warming and inviting-
Yet, momentarily, it's something to behold

A simple kiss
A warm embrace
A familiarity in my heart
Let me know that you are still there

I come home just to feel you here

Alisha Williams
What She Had In Her Purse

From her purse
As she fished around the bottom,
I waited, patiently.
Wait just a minute, she'd say.
And so, I did.
Grandma,
Can't move as fast as
She used to,
With a grin.
It never failed,
From the bottom of her purse,
She made magic,
She pulled the sweetest treat of all,
With my hand open,
She placed within my eager hand,
A soft peppermint.

Willetta J. Davis
To Be Unexpected

I was not expecting you
But I did not expect for you to leave so soon
Or at all
I was excited, yet, afraid at the same time
But, mostly excited to know-
You would be here one day soon
And be all mine
To hold you in my arms
To smell the sweetness is what I was looking forward to

But God only knows why he had to keep you.

Kimberly Monique Smith
Jessica Lyn
A Mother's Imagine

I adore her face as she looked up at me wondering if she knew I'm the one who's been waiting for her.

I lean close to smell her breath that sweetened my spirit and refreshed my heart.

As I placed her hand in mine searching for a resemblance;

I felt her tiny hand gently caress mine which brought a sense of peace to every part of me.

I imagined the first time she opened her beautiful brown eyes and recognized me as her mommy; my heart burst with such love it felt unnatural.

Everything I desired to know about love was established through her.

I noticed her smiling and I wondered why is she smiling? Could it be the angels singing to her or was it because of me, her mommy and the love she felt from me?

I aesthetically realized it was both and my spirit was at ease.

I imagine counting her tiny fingers and toes making sure they were all there; the exuberance of rubbing her soft feet on my face became my heavenly lyric only for her.

I imagine the moment I heard her first sweet cry and thinking how happy I was to know what my little angel needed from me.

The calmness I felt as I watched her sleep at night; a sweetness only a mother could imagine.

Feeling the rhythm of her breathing join with mine, only happiness a mother could imagine.

I imagine brushing the soft curls of my angel's hair, the smoothness of her skin, the dimples in her cheeks, and the radiance in her eyes only a Mother could adore.

My Jessica Lyn, my beautiful blessings from God.

A Mother's Imagine and Love

Alisha Williams
Ms. Ethel's Grateful Heart

Ms. Ethel sat up in the bed
For the fourth time
She looked at the clock
With what felt like the twelfth time,
 She reached over to grab the phone
But she sat back against her
headboard.
Okay, she said,
"Don't call."
She put the phone back on the hook
And pulled the ruffled covers up
To her chin.
Her house seemed
To be extremely silent
She shrunk back down
Into the covers hoping that
The warmness from her covers
would somehow comfort her.
But to no avail.
"I'm not going to call them again."
She thought,
Even though,
Arizona was a great distance away,
"They should be here by now."
She'd only called a dozen times
Before she went to bed.
She thought about all the things
That could have gone wrong.
Then, between flashes of their faces
And her praying,
She fell asleep.

What seemed like seconds
But what was really three hours
She felt light on her face
She slowly opened her eyes to see
That the sun had risen.
She told herself,
Joy comes in the morning light,
She listened intently
For life scurrying in the
House,
She heard not a sound,
She threw herself out of bed,
Slipped on her house shoes,
And went right downstairs,
One house shoe got caught
On the steps,
She looked down to
Scold it before she slipped it back on,
She looked up,
Before her mouth could speak,
Her eyes were exceedingly glad.
Her heart spilled out gratefulness.
She saw, there on the couch
With their coats still on
Was her brother, and her daughter
Home from college.
She sighed within herself.
Smiled a great big smile,
And tiptoed back upstairs
With a heart bursting with gratefulness.
Careful not to wake them.

I wrote this song for my Mother on her first day of chemotherapy after her diagnosis of breast cancer in 2011. My mother was worried and almost horrified of chemo. I sat in that lobby as they prepped her in the back and thought about what she would say to me. You see, I was a hypochondriac when I was younger, and she would tell me to stop worrying about things. In October 2011 I found myself saying the same thing...

Willetta J. Davis

To Mama:
DON'T WORRY ABOUT IT
Chorus:
Don't worry about it/ Everything will be alright/ You don't have to doubt it/ 'Cause we are healed by His stripes/ Just go ahead and shout it/ I am strong and I have faith/ I will survive today
Verse 1:
I gave up on life/ I didn't want to face it/ My diagnosis wasn't right/ I didn't want to fight it/ Anxiety had taken over me/ I didn't think I could be/ (the woman)/ Who I use to be/ Then a friend told me/ I need to believe/ (in Him)/ and stop letting the enemy/ lie, steal, and deceive me/ and live my life/ you have to live your life and...
        (Repeat Chorus)
Verse 2:
Now I'm living my life/ There's no doubt about it/ Jesus already paid the price/ I just want to shout/ Yes/ I want to thank you Lord/ for healing me/ 'Cause I was so lost and too blind/ to see your grace and mercy/ (You see)/ a friend told me/ I need to believe/ (in Him)/ and stop letting the enemy/ lie, steal, and deceive me/ and live my life/ I had to live my life and...

Don't worry about it

Chapter Four

SERENIITY

Jeslyn Lewis

Peace of Mind

Old school music, rhythm and rhyme:

These things describe my peace of mind.

Smiles from my children, quality time;

What more do I need to have peace of mind?

Pastel colored flowers, a little sunshine;

These things added for some peace to find.

Besties and loved ones, the ties that bind;

All blended together gives me peace of mind.

Making others happy is a definite sign,

That truly deep down inside, I have peace of mind!

One simple gift, I can never decline,

Is one of life's purest pleasures called, peace of mind.

Worries and sorrows all left behind,

Today is my first day discovering true peace of mind!

J.M. Perkins

UnWine

In starting your morning with affirmations and inspirations in hopes that grace and mercies is your destination

You fight with traffic, trying to yield your tongue as someone cuts you off and jumps in front of you from the third left lane only to exit far right

You regain your composure and state of mind as you place on your meditations from your favorite play list on Pandora

You finally arrive at your job. You love your job but hate management. So, you say another prayer before getting out of the car.

You struggle through the day changing faces, faking it because you still haven't made it, smiling and even eating a huge plate called, "kiss butt," for lunch.

You're uneasy in your spirit as you discuss with your family and your loved ones about how crappy your job is, all day. Incoming and outgoing calls.

You can't wait till the end of your day but those last 30 minutes' drags like Linus blanket.

Finally, the time has come for you to clock out. As you start on your way, you're hoping your travel home is a bit more therapeutic than your travel to work.

Unfortunately, 5 o'clock track shows you no mercy, and it's just not going to happen.

You press on anyways as your family is waiting on you at home. You arrive at home. Although you are happy to be there, you remain outside to de-stress for another 45 minutes.

You can smell the aroma of the food as you walk towards the door. Dinner awaits you. And as your loved one pour you a glass of your favorite wine you try your best to UnWine.

UnWine your mind from traffic and work. UnWine your body as you wash off the days' work and bad vibes. Just let it go and UnWine.

Kimberly Monique Smith
The Night

The night felt strange to me; it was a lonely night. The wind was blowing against my window sounding like voices. I immediately rose to the height of the noise. As I closely listened, I notice the leaves from the shrubs swaying back and forth as if they were speaking to me. I stared at them for a moment wondering if they could speak what would they say. Would they reveal to me of all the things they saw during the day and night? Or would they be silent as they should be? Would they tell me of the nights when I heard voices it was God commanding them to silence my hearing when I felt afraid, or enhance it when I was at ease? Opening my eyes, I watched the leaves that swayed back and forth, up and down reminding me of the sound of harp music with its magnificent rhythm. The reflection as the wind blew and the images God allowed me to see. The stems of the leaves were running in circles like children playing in an open field on a sunny windy day and their laughter echoing in the air. As I admired their freedom of movement, I closed my eyes again and softly mouthed "Thank You God", for your creation and the mind of imagination.

Willetta J. Davis

VISION

I see my future ahead of me
Because my right now
Presently-
is not where I want to be.
So I'll glance at it just to see
the mistakes I have made (some too deep)
and know not to carry them with me
On my way to my destiny
We are not promised tomorrow
But I refuse to sit here in sorrow –
Sitting and sulking about today
But instead I'll have hope and will for tomorrow
Knowing that Almighty God has already made a way for me
On my way to my destiny
Life is but a dream
They say
And though today did not go the way that I had planned
I know now to let go of my life and put it in God's hand
You see, too many times our vision is tunneled
Because we dig the horizontal hole
Unable to let go of our past and the mistakes that we made
yesterday
That our todays show signs of "NO WAYS"
Giving up on hopes and dreams – a brighter tomorrow
So caught up with disappointments, suffering, pain and
sorrow
Feeling hollow-
Empty
Tunnel vision is not the diagnosis for me
I refuse to be put under
Only seeing what is in front of me

Keeping my peripheral, spherical vision clear-
Clearly
Never looking down
I'm upward bound
I'm an overachiever
A victorious believer
Holy Ghost scholar-
make me want to holler
"I can do all things through Christ that strengthens me
That no weapon formed against me shall prosper"
And no matter what I'm going through I'll play my role as a
Godstar
Knowing that I'm blessed and highly favored
I'll sing my praises so wonderful and beautifully
I'll be #1 on the praise party
Earning my G.R.A.M.M.Y.
(God Redeemed All My Mistakes, Yes)
Because I am too blessed to be stressed
I don't have time for no "woe is me" type of mess
I don't have time for no pity party
I'm going to the one that raises, uplift, glorify and praise His
name
Because my vision is 20/20 strong.
Seeing today's lesson as tomorrow's blessings
Moving on
Canceling out all my wrongs
Stay tuned there is more to come and more to see
As I Thank God for today and walk into my destiny

Jeslyn Lewis
Prosperity

Although it is prevalent,

many miss it as they pursue the twin,

otherwise known as, success.

The greedy seek to devour it,

the humble strive for a healthy courtship with it.

Though it is not an easy find,

with hard work, determination, and creativity,

it is a viable option; and yes, it is available.

Sought out, thought out;

matriculated, vindicated...

never abbreviated

All or nothing is the motto!

It reaches beyond,

bends backwards,

and stretches forth!

It is a part of the human race;

it is the blessing waiting to be obedient~

It is called prosperity!

Have some...

Alisha Williams
Mother Said

Stand right there sweetie
Right here?
Yes, Right there
and let the sun hit your face
Feel it, embrace it
The forecast for today
It's sunny with a chance of happy
No clouds,
No rain,
Just breathe for once
And take in the oxygen
That illuminates the beauty of your own skin
Hold your head up
There is nothing to be ashamed of
Lots of people have
Went rounds of bouts with love
And got knocked down for the count
But the difference is
When the ref said
10, the will inside you struggles
9, can it be done?
8, no, just stay down
7, you will not make it
6, I got to fight
5, feeling your strength now
4, pray even harder and keep going
3, stirring around, might even fall back down
2, getting to your knees now, finding your footing
1 get back up start to moving
That's it sugar, keep looking up
That Man above got you.
Now, don't give up.

Willetta J. Davis

Never

Never give up on your dreams
Even though it may seem too high to reach or too hard to get to
Your dreams are your multi-million-dollar realities waiting for you
Never give up

Never give up on your dreams
Even when the dream snatchers tell you-
"Your dreams, are impossible to do."
Just know they are just lost souls on deserted roads
Who once had dreams themselves that they too, did not believe
could come true
Never give up

Never give up on your dreams
Keep it on your mind
Instill it in your heart
Embed it deep down in your soul
Stop half living the dreams of others
Start living your dreams that make you whole
Your dreams are your passions
Your passions are your actions
Your actions are the reactions of dreams fulfilled
Plus, a life lived with satisfaction

Multiply your dreams, add faith and subtract the doubt
In a fraction of time, your dreams will equal out

Yesterday you believed
Today you will achieve
Tomorrow you shall succeed
And watch all your dreams become your new reality
Never give up

Never give up on your dreams
Like Dr. Martin Luther King, Jr. who –
Shared his dreams with many nations
Planted seeds of HOPE, CHANGE, and DETERMINATION
Impacted the lives of ALL generations
Never gave up on his dreams

Never give up on your dreams
Like Jessie who plowed the field of HOPE
And kept HOPE alive
Declaring I AM SOMEBODY with his eyes on the prize
Put determination in the eyes of a man in Chicagoland
Who built his dreams on HOPE, CHANGE and…
YES, WE CAN!
And is still moving forward with his dreams to build a better
nation!
Never give up

Never give up on your dreams
Even though it may seem too high to reach or too hard to get to
Yes, the enemy is going to try to attack you!
But, "no weapon formed against you shall prosper."
Believe-
Because it is true

Sometimes the road may not be easy
Sometimes it may even hurt
But, don't get discouraged DREAM MAKERS
Yet, seek the KINGDOM first!

Even when you think you can't
GOD knows you can
So, keep on DREAMING and BELIEVING
Philippians 4:13-
I can do ALL things through Christ that strengthens ME!
NEVER GIVE UP!

Chapter Five

The Art of...
Being Me

Jeslyn Lewis

Introducing Ms. Pensational Imagery

Big, attainable, unstoppable...my dreams

Dark, exotic, untold...my secrets

Heartfelt, gut-wrenching, tearjerker...my story

Writing, relating, ministry...my passion

Life, love, laughter...my mission

Beauty, miracles, blessings...my inspiration

Collective, bold, expressive...my writing

Mediocre, fluctuating, rising...my confidence

Exposed, naked, wholesome...my soul

Damaged, broken, repairable...my heart

Missing pieces, curve balls, winding roads...my life

Omnipotent, Omnipresent, Omniscient...my Hope

Real, tangible, genuine...Jeslyn, Ms. Pensational Imagery

Jeslyn Lewis

Funny, Ain't It?

Ain't it funny how for some folks the color of my skin predicts my altitude?
Funny how when I clothe myself in self-confidence, it's called an attitude?
Ain't it funny how all eyes are on the gentle sway of my wide hips?
Funny how I'm considered "ghetto" until I open my colored glossed lips?
Ain't it funny how I have to be over qualified or have two or more degrees?
Funny how even though I'm denied a fair chance, I still aim to please?
Ain't it funny how the lighter my shade, ha-ha-ha, the better my grade?
Funny how a lite complexion, silky hair, and thin lips have it "almost" made?
Ain't it funny how I am blessed, bright, brilliant, and beautiful from the inside out~
Funny how even when they shake my hand, my credentials they still doubt?
Ain't it funny how my best is not quite good enough; my 100% requires an additional whole?
Funny how if I sell my soul, hahaha, I'm suddenly worth my weight in gold?
Ain't it funny that my ambition is acknowledged as an unattainable dream?
Funny how I am viewed as a threat because I say just what I mean?
But I'll keep on dancing on blue eyed devil's head;
I am Blessed, Black, Brilliant, and Beautiful, and that in itself, hahaha, is enough said!!!

Willetta J. Davis

Folk

(From: Lette's Talk Before I Go Crazy)

Lettie: *(She is sitting on the porch fanning herself. She is irritated and showing a lot of attitude: Waving her hands in the air, rolling her eyes and neck, smacking and twisting her lips. Lettie talks fast so you must keep up!)*

People… or should I say FOLK amazzzzze me! It's funny how "folk"- old folk, young folk, kin folk…just any ol' folk, can ALWAYS find failure in ANYTHING, EVERYTHING, and sometimes NOTHING you do!

For instance: *(pointing her finger as if she is about to make a point)* If you come up with an idea or an opportunity to do something and it wasn't their idea OR if that idea or opportunity wasn't anything they had interested in EVER doing (huh) OR if it wasn't THEIR plan for you- it's the WRONG idea or opportunity! (DoN't YoU HaTe ThAt?!?)

Have you EVER wondered why this or that is so? It's because………………*(rolls her neck and eyes)* IT'S NOT THEIR IDEA!! "The Folk" did NOT come up with it.

It's funny how The Folk will find EVERY WAY to convince you out of your plans or better yet your "Calling". And…what I've come to find out over the years is that the WORST ones are the "Scriptural Justifiers" you know, aka "Bible Thumpers". *(thumps the middle of her hands)*

It's sooooo funny how folk "the Scriptural ones" can find EVERY scripture in the Bible that tells YOU what you are about to do is going to fail you. *(rolls neck and eyes while shaking finger side to side)* BUT, they can NEVER, EVER *find* that scripture that tells you how you are going to succeed at it- how "I can do all things through Christ that strengthens me" or how "no weapon formed against me shall prosper". But they can find those words that are like weapons of DIScouragement that cuts through your skin like a whip or dagger- biting your skin and killing your flesh, torturing your soul?

Where is that scripture that tells you Jesus will never set you up to fail? Yet, He sets you up to learn to be successful? Where are the scriptures that says even IF I FALL or FAIL, just have FAITH! Because Faith will NEVER FAIL you?

(Stands up and begin swaying from side to side as if she is in the choir)

Whoa...Ohhh...Ohhh...Ohhh...Ohh/ can't turn around/we've come this far by Faith? ***(Waves hand in the air)***

YES!!

Where are those scriptures FOLK... that tells you to acknowledge Him first in ALL things? Where are those scriptures that tells you that He will carry you? Where are THOSE scriptures? It's funny how they NEVER find those scriptures. You can't depend on FOLK!

You have to: *Ask the Savior to help you/hmmmmm...hmm...hmmmmm...hmm...hmmmm you/ naaaaa...nanana....naaaaa...nanana youuu/ He will carry you through/*

YESSS!!

"Folk" ...old folk, young folk, kin folk amazzzzzzes me! Folk are funny (yes, they are). It's funny how with folk, you are the one who is setting yourself up for failure, but in for real, for real, reality, realistically, realness, it's "The Folk" who are your set-up? (hmmmm). One minute they tell you ALL the reasons you "Ain't and you cain't, ain't no way, "no shows" yesterdays, todays and tomorrows?

 BUT wait! *(hold hand up in the halt position)* When you do SUCCEED at YOUR hopes, dreams, plans, ideas and opportunities...THE same OL' FOLK who were so quick to tell the HOW, WHO, WHAT, WHEN and WHY you can't succeed...are the first ones to tell you how they always knew you were going to make it one day (with that money in your pockets?)

SOME FOLK- I tell you!!!

Note to self: STOP LISTENING TO FOLK!! SEEK GOD FIRST!! HE WILL NEVER FAIL YOU!

Quote: Folk are quick to tell you how you are not going to succeed than how you will succeed. Know the difference!!

Willetta J. Davis
...They Said

They said I was too little-
That I wasn't tall enough

They said I was too weak-
That I wasn't tough
Or had the right stuff

They said that I wasn't pretty-
I just did not have the looks

They said I was too skinny-
That I needed to eat everything that was cooked

But then they said I was too fat
What's up with THAT?

They said I wasn't that smart-
That I just didn't have the skills

They said I didn't know how to talk-
Intellectually or intelligently...

But I say...
TO HELL WITH WHAT THEY SAY!

Because I have the POWER
That has the WILL

And Mother said....

Willetta J. Davis

...and Mother Said

Raise your' head my child'
You have nothing to be ashamed of
Their lives "ain't" no better than yours-
It never will be
Because it never was

Hold your head high my dear
Higher than the sun that shines so bright-
Let it be seen
Let it be known
You are the fruit
You are the light

Walk proudly on this Earth
Oh, Beautiful One
All the days of your life-

Step high with dignity
And let the Spirit be your guide

And Big Mama Said...

Willetta J. Davis
SANG!

Keep a song in yo'. heart to drown out ALL that negativity.
Only fools sing songs so foolishly.
Sang chil' sang...
Sang chil' sang!

Free yo' mind...free yo' soul
Free yo' mind...free yo' soul
Free yo' mind...free yo' soul

Keep a song in yo' heart
Don't be a half ass being
Be smart and remain whole.

Sang chil' sang
La...de...da...la...de...da...de...da

Sang chil' sang
Sang chil'...
Free yo' soul, chil'
And...

SANG!

Willetta J. Davis

PUSH, GO, FLOW (From the Blackman's Corner)

PUSH
Push
Puuushhh on my Brother
DON'T STOP
KEEP GOING!

GO
Go
Goooooo on my SISTER
KEEP THE FAITH
KEEP FLOWING!

FLOW
Flow
Flooowww on my People
STAND UP
EXTEND YOUR POWER

And say…

RIGHT ON!

Jeslyn Lewis
Imagine the World without Us

How dare they try to count us out~
Just pretend that beyond the shadow of a doubt~
That we, the brown skinned heirs of the throne,
Dissipate, vacate and Just...be gone!
Without us...
The survivors of massacres, the strong towers that petition the
Unseen Face;
The ones who are intimately connected with faith, mercy, and
grace~
The we, who hold up the banners and endure until the end of the
race~
The us, who keep the balance by maneuvering at a steady pace~
Without us...there would be indescribable mayhem!
How dare they insinuate that we contribute to nothingism, when
In fact, we diversify the field known as professionism~
Even though we are profiled and denied we still break down
barriers;
We are the future, we justify the means and promote dream
carriers!
Without us...there would be inexplicable pandemonium!
We contribute to the evisceration of gloom, with our bright
personalities;
Our genuine finesse, our open minds and constant struggle for
more versatility!
We realize the need for more diversity, we see the significance for
multiplicity~
We believe in options, so we have upgraded from simplicity and
mediocrity!
Without us...there would be inconceivable disorder!
Without us...
Without the ones who define struggle and continue onward in spite
of;
Without the chosen, the generation of brazen prizes who win just
because of;

Without the thoroughbred nation, the beginning of beauty~
 those who persevere in lieu of
Without the go getters, the fighters, the movers, shakers and money
makers,the champions, the trendsetters and trailblazers, the peace
seekers, the top notchers and head honchos who prevail instead
of~
Without us...there would be incomprehensible outrage!
Please tell me, where would the world be...without us?
I think about these things and I laugh because~
How dare they try to count us out~
Just pretend that beyond the shadow of a doubt~
That we, the brown skinned heirs of the throne,
Dissipate, vacate and poof...be gone

Because without us...
THEY wouldn't have a snowball's chance in hell...
Not Without US

Kimberly Monique Smith
The Mirror

The girl said, Mirror! Mirror! In my heart, why do you make me cry?

I talk to you when I feel pretty, and when I am alone with you in the dark.

You said, pick me up whenever you need encouragement and I will be there to make you smile.

But when I look at you, mirror, you close your face within. Mirror! Mirror! Why do you make me cry?

The mirror answered, Girl! Girl! In my face, why do you need me to make you smile? I am just a piece of glass you hold in your hand or hang on a wall; your beauty does not lie within my reflection, but in the image of your heart.

Girl! Girl! In my face, turn away from me; for what I see, you should see is your beauty from the reflection of your heart.

Mirror! Mirror! Thank you, thank you for I finally see what you see; I see the beauty of the reflection of my heart and not of you. My reflection is in the eye of the beholder, which is me; the only one that truly matters are the images of my heart.

Willetta J. Davis
Sunflower's Song

I am a Sunflower
Planted in Winter's bliss
Nurtured by Nature
Rooted in the Earth
Dignified and strong
Painted with natural beauty
Admired near and far
A passion for my Lovers
Cherished in every heart
A dancer in the wind
A songstress of Jazz
Full of class-
Rapturous and free
I bathe beneath the stars
And embrace the moon
The new day brings new melodic tunes
I lay under the sun as its warmth comforts me
Sit under the trees
Enjoy the cool breeze-
As the sway of the leaves and song of the blue birds
Entices me with its soulful melodies
While making love to the Honeybees

Jeslyn Lewis
Black Girls Rock

Gentlemen, I'm going to talk to the sistahs for a minute because
trust me, I got y'all next!

Sistahs, let's vibe for a moment okay?
Our Black is so undeniably BEAUTIFUL~
It ain't a sin to be comfortable in the skin that you're in!
When the bruthas see us, all they see is assets and dividends.
So whether you are dark chocolate, caramel, or a creamy white
chocolate...
There's just something about that melanin
Black girl, You rock! Bu-lee dat, know dat...
show dat and flow dat
because you are dat

Embrace who you are from the crown of your beautiful head
to the soles of your JesLovely feet...
we are the victory, because we don't accept defeat
so
Love   your   skin,
every single mouth-watering inch of it-
When the enemy tries to hate on you it's totally irrelevant!
That face that displays a smile that can work any room~
We are the tick tock of clock, and the dynamite's boom~
Our neck serves as a vase for that crown full of intellect and
wisdom
Breasts full of nourishment, life, and yes enticement!
A dribble drabble dribble of wondrous enrichment~
Behind those voluptuous breasts is a heart of pure gold,
a heart filled with enough love to heal the whole world-
The very soul to soul of stories untold...
Sistahs...
Our arms were built to hold and comfort~
Every tribe this nation has to offer.
A belly from which the living water freely

flows and flows and flows-
We provide sustenance and help others grow~
And that ain't the only rivers we produce!
Yeah we're just that bad or didn't you know?
Thighs that disguise the surprise... no need to compromise the prize!
Real eyes realize the conquest of our sighs, the lows and especially the highs~
Legs that sustain the weight of all that treasure we carry around each and every day~
Sistahs what chu say? Impose, exposed, our silent woes,
Whatever be the case, it's worth it!
Feet that leave footprints in the sands of time;
Best believe we fine...
And don't let us unwind and refine all the pleasures we are naturally born with
A gift, with a gift, carried by a gift, breeding gifts, gifted!
We gotta keep each other lifted...

We snap, crackle, and like firecrackers we pop;
From the bottom to the tip top, we don't stop
Because sistahs we rockety rock rock rock!
When we ain't poppin, we sit and sparkle~
Dazzling as we bedazzle, refusing the shackles
Honeysuckle smelling, honey flavored... with just a hint of spicy!
We are the true definition of nicety!
Beautiful Black Queens who change the course of the wind;
No such thing as failure, we live to win, win, win...
outside and within~
With all the riches we house within
our beautiful black selves
We are the trophy too heavy for shelves!
They ain't ready for our level of mother wit,
our age-old wisdom, and our born intellect~
They don't like it, but must respect it!
Never neglect it, always protect it!

By any means necessary-
damn the adversary
This blackness that is unrivaled, comparable to none;
Complete, whole, beautiful, blessed, bossy,
Chosen, sacred, beneficial, essential,
privately owned and operated
Sistahs Embrace it NOW-
our perfect imperfections, our unembellished flaws;
By showing the world that
OUR BLACK IS SO Undeniably BEAUTIFUL
Simply because
Black girls rock
Black girls rock and we don't stop-
Sing it with me now~
Black girls rock and we don't stop!

Chapter Six

P.S. LOVE

Willetta J. Davis
Love Is

Love is patient

Love is kind

It's not envious, boastful, proud, rude or has a selfish mind

It's not easily angered, keeps no records of wrongs-

 nor delight in evil

But rejoices with truth all the day long

Love always protects, trust, hopes and preserves

Love never fails

Love never falls

Love is victorious

Love conquers all

Everlasting love

Love lasting forever

Never giving up on love because love will keep us together

In our hearts love will forever stay

Because love never fades or can be washed away

Love is here for eternity, indefinitely, living in you and me

Not easily broken
Love is bold and clear to see

Love is blind- not discriminating
Love teaches us to love all our enemies
Love covers all wrongs
It is the defeat to hate
For God is Love and-
Love is great

Greater is He that is in me-
That's Love
The greatest of them all
The first Fruit of the Spirit to be called

Love is the fulfilment of the laws
Perfectly polished with no flaws
A perfect love does not fear
It drives fear completely out
And because of His perfect love
I will have no doubt

Love does not lie, steal, or cheat
But love is filled with trust, giving and honesty

Love is sincere

Love does not harm

Love is real

 Unlike its pretense- Charm

"Putting on" love with words and tongue

Yet, put on love like Solomon in Songs and David in Psalms

Bear with one another in love

Love deeply as a mother loves her child

Teaching them in all things to love the Lord

To walk in His ways

Holding fast to Him all the while

Husbands love your wives

As He loves the church and himself

Wives respect your husbands

Coveting no one else

Above all things love the Lord with all your heart

And

Love your neighbor as yourself

I love the Lord

He is my strength and my salvation

I love the Lord

He heard my cry throughout all the nations

For God so loved the world that He gave his only Son

That whoever believed in Him shall not perish

But shall have everlasting life

Bearing all our sins and burdens

Healing us by His stripes

There is no greater Love than He who lay down his life for a friend

And what a friend we have in Jesus

A friend who always loves

Now until the end...

Jesus loves me this I know

For the Bible tells me so

And

Oh, how I love Jesus

Because He first loved me

Alisha Williams
Your Overcoming Love

You whisper, preserve, my love.
If it had not been for You.
I would not have the will to go on.
But your love assures me
You are with me
Rain, sleet, shine, or through any storm.
Your Word is true.
For I know the plans
I have for you,"
declares the LORD, "
plans to prosper you
and not to harm you,
plans to give you hope and a future.
Jeremiah 29:11
Your love is pure Heaven.
You have carried me.
Seeded hope into me.
You have kept me.
You have wrapped me in Your Love
Your love Heavenly Father God
Draws me close.
Keep us near,
In Your blossoms we do declare,
You are worthy of all praise
Today, forever, everyday always.

Willetta J. Davis
Where There Is Love

Where there is love

There is forgiving and forgetting

Honoring and respecting

Cherishing and Understanding

No commanding and demanding

Where there is love...

There is comforting and nourishing

Prosperity and flourishing

Mending and molding

Supporting and upholding

Where there is love...

There is giving and caring

Committing and sharing

Sacrificing and suffering

Believing and trusting

Where there is love...

Temptation is passing

Where there is love...

Love is everlasting

Jeslyn Lewis
Life, Love, & Lemons

I love you right now, not by happen stance,

but because I want to~

Life has issued me my share of lemons

And for a long time,

I didn't understand how to add

An icy attitude, a sugary smile

and call it lemonade

I just ate the lemons, lemon peels and all.

That was until I met you;

Now it feels as if it's springtime in my life;

The flowers are blooming,

the birds are chirping,

The bees are buzzing, and

the wind is whisking through my hair.

I am at peace with life;

 I am one with the universe

I love you right now, not by happen stance,

but because I want to.

Jeslyn Lewis

Ocean

Standing on the shoreline, looking out at the ocean

No lifeguard, no life jacket...

Just me, my dreams, and my heart in hand

I see you, miles away from me

I call to you... softly

With tears in my eyes I bid you to come to the shore for me

Waves carry you further out, crashing upon you... beating you

I feel every pain you feel

As tears ease down my face

I place one foot into the waters that I believe will soon overtake me too

I lunge forward because I see you steadily drifting further and further away

I cast myself upon a dream and will myself to you

The currents come against me, vigorously

Instinctively I begin to fight the waters, the battle is pointless

Then a vision of you comes to mind and I am calmed

Out of nowhere I feel your arms around my waist

You hold me captive until I realize I am not dreaming

You are there

I was coming to save you

But you, you came for me, came to me, came to my rescue even when you needed saving

Together, eyes locked on the lighthouse, we swim to the shore

Caught up in our own world, we love each other so completely until in that moment

We are healed, we are found, we become one!

Willetta J. Davis
reception

you opened your arms to me
i entered like a curious child through an open door
and there I nestled my head upon your chest
and buried all my fears of being alone
as you closed me into your embrace of love

we danced all night at your uncle's wedding
exchanging passionate caresses
falling into each other's eyes
loving-
living in each other's arms
reminiscing about the first time we made love

when the music ended
and the lights were shut off
there we stayed locked in each other's soul
never letting go

we kissed
and knew we were in love

Jeslyn Lewis
More than Enough

In the distance I feel you watching me;

Your eyes are on my flesh like a sweet whisper on my skin.

I feel you getting closer to me;

Your look tells me, "no touching!"

As I dream of nights spent in your arms,

My breathing becomes altered~

I see the strength that is about to envelope me!

No not the natural strength from pumping iron,

But that fortitude from kneeling before Him who made us free~

I dare not shy away from you, although slightly intimidated

By the words not spoken~

I am somehow drawn to the man behind your face.

I see so much more than you allow me to see;

I see the prayers of the righteous coming to fruition~

I see the usurping of past sorrows~

I see the reshaping of that man in the mirror~

I see you, the real you, the you that you are on your way to becoming.

I see you and a warm sensation rushes over me;

I become excited,

My heartbeat accelerates as I stand before my Adam, my King David, my Moses

My unembellished flaw, my wholesome wholeness;

My tamed savage; my cool heat;

My mighty prayer warrior, my spoken word;

My push forward, my leap of faith;

My baptizing flood, my reviving life water;

My mountaintop experience, my valley spring;

My now, my still, my always

My more than enough~

Willetta J. Davis
Eve Speaks

Lust hangs from the branch of the forbidden tree in the Garden of Eden
I am tempted to taste its forbidden sweetness
My lips quiver with anticipation of its round
My tongue tingles with desperation
I close my eyes tasting its imaginative juices
I swallow my imagination
I am tempted with sensation
I open my eyes and approach my passion
With admiration of its wholeness
My tempestuous desires dare me to touch it
My fingertips burn
My flesh yearns
My conscious warns
I ignore and pluck it from its base
Igniting my mouth with the forbidden
Savoring its sinful taste

Alisha Williams
Good Gardening

Just what if I let him hold me
What if those feelings of emotions start to swell, the ones my heart
started to miss
The ones that embraced you and nothing else to follow
Feelings of a game being played
Moving chess pieces with strings
Cut the strings then tie them back together
Hoping they don't come apart at the ends
Some say love is a gamble is it not
Or is it leaving too much to chance
What if it's real?
Could it be?
I mean,
I thought it was before?
It was real for me, at least.
Besides,
Feelings are fickle
And facts or fading
Waiting
On what?
On the truth of him to show up
Smooth away the anxiety with one touch
Keep your clothes on
Just smile for me, yes
That's enough
The way the light hit you just right
But without it you still glow,
That part, yeah
where you become my unison.
Just rest
That's all I require
That is the ultimate test
That's love
When you can sense your partners

Needs without them saying it
When you can lay
And sex doesn't even cross your mind
Instead you spend it
Learning quirky details that no one else knew
Funny how love grows underneath
Like the stems bursting out of seeds
Into the fertile ground
Watered with laughter, and silly antics
Seriously, Get beneath the surface man
Who are you really?
Plant your seeds in my heart
Watch them grow
And choke out every bad seed that was
Previously sown.

Jeslyn Lewis
NAKED*

Naked I stand before you, nervous, trembling, unsure...

With my eyes, I call out to you.

My eyes say words I could never utter, begging, pleading, needing, hoping, wishing, praying.

You approach me slowly, cautiously, willingly.

You reach out to me and loosely drape yourself about my head for the purpose of protecting my thoughts and I, well I trust them to you alone.

You accessorize the excellence of my beauty; you do not draw attention away from my attributes, I wear you well.

Around my neck, feather lightly you lie; your desire not to fit to snugly and cause me alarm.

Gently you caress the scars left by the previous ensemble I wore.

With the security of a breastplate but breathable allowing the utmost comfort~

sheltering my readily aroused nipples tenderly clinging to them massaging each one ever so often to remind me that you are still there aiming to tease and willing to please.

Freely you hang about my abdominal area.

You know my weaknesses and feel my complexes.

You recognize my insecurities about the wounds left by the flames on the fleshy incubator of my heritage, my womb inhabitants.

The blaze imprints are a constant reminder of why I have to keep my torch lit.

And my seedlings, my seedlings are my motivation and I must carry the torch in their honor.

You care for me and assist in nurturing them as they are an integral part of me.

While I am sleeping, I feel you softly touching me there, tracing the lines of my burn sites, consoling me, comforting my anxiety, reassuring me that you are ever with me even in my sleep and the scorched area stings no more as you repair the singes.

Your touch promotes healing and extinguishes the after burn.

I wear you well.

Firmly you hang around my hips, the constant sway massaging your manhood exciting you to the point that you yearn to move away but helpless you remain...motionless.

Securely hugging my thighs offering support to yet another weakness; the tightness of your fit to me leaves me feeling slightly relieved.

The fact that you hug me there, breeds strength, enhances confidence and raises my level of awareness of your actually being there!

You soothe me by loving my flaws more intensely than the rest of me.

You never reach for my legs...you stay clear of my calves.

They accentuate our solidarity.

You enclose all of me except my flawed virtue; you choose to leave it untouched.

You are my garment!

You modulate my behavior, you cover me with your love, envelope me with your manhood, surround me with your strength and favor me with your touch.

The sacred place bearing my jewel, you refuse to infiltrate yet you willingly inhale my sweet nectar.

The purity of my flawed virtue is the miracle you wish to savor and preserve.

You are my garment you complete me, you compliment me and I wear you well!!!

You, my love are my garment!!!

Willetta J. Davis

You're My Inspiration (Song)

This was one of the first songs that I had written for our group P.S. Love. I believe I was about 13years old. It was inspired by a boy I saw at the Natchitoches Festival of Lights back in the 1980's. HE WAS CUTE!

1st Verse:

Boy/ the way I feel about you/ is a feeling/ I never had before/ Yet not knowing what love really is/ I'm glad I found it in you

Chorus

You're /my inspiration/ You're my inspiration/ You're/ my inspiration

2nd Verse

Baby/ this love I have for you/so deep inside of me / is all so true/ and when I'm with you, boy/ you turn my whole life around/ and I'm so glad you're the one I found

Willetta J. Davis

You're My Inspiration (Poem)

The way I feel about you is a feeling I've never had before
You've opened my eyes to many things
And showed me that "love" is just not a word but so much more
You give me love
Good love
Sweet love
Eternal love
And allowed me to give it back to you
You make me feel loved
Showered me with so much love
There is nothing in this world I wouldn't do
To show you the love you give to me
Is special in so many ways that are true

This love I have for you
Burns deep inside
It's like an eternal flame
This smile you've put on my face will never go away
Every time I'm with you-
Every time I'm near you
You turn my whole world around
I'm floating on clouds
Soaring through the skies
Embracing this precious love, we've found

You're my inspiration
My sweet sensation
And this dedication is for you

Jeslyn Lewis

All I Want... is Love

I want a wake up with only me on his mind kinda love;

A anytime is the right time kinda love!

I want a anywhere you touch me is that spot kinda love;

A touch that's always hot kinda love.

I want a bring me breakfast in bed kinda love;

A toast, juice, pancakes, grits and eggs kinda love.

I want a meet me at 12, have me for lunch kinda love;

A bring yo kids to meet my kids we have a Brady bunch kinda love.

I want a there's nothing you can't tell me kinda love;

A no more being in this old shell kinda love.

I want a wake up at midnight and let's pray kinda love;

A kiss all my tears away kinda love;

I want a paint a rainbow and you name the colors after me kinda love;

A let's lay on the hammock between two trees kinda love.

I want a it's okay to like it rough kinda love;

A I'll be by your side when the goings get tough kinda love.

I want a dance by the water when there's no music playing kinda love;

A I'll love you forever is what I'm saying kinda love.

I want a write me a love song only my heart can hear kinda love;

A whatever is wrong I'll lend you my ear kinda love.

I want a we feel each other's pain kinda love;

A nothing can sever us cause we twain kinda love.

I want a discretionary slap me on my butt in the public kinda love;

A if they looking so what, kinda love.

I want a all through the day kiss me on my forehead kinda love;

A we don't always do it in the bed kinda love!

I want a carry my heart in your heart kinda love;

A let's begin where ever we start kinda love.

I want a enjoy the black, white, and gray areas kinda love;

A yellow pink purple and green day kinda love.

I want a just us two, me and you kinda love;

A bring the kids over, we'll find something to do kinda love.

I want a I can trust you with my friends kinda love;

A we're pals until the very end kinda love.

I want a let's play in the rain kinda love;

A make the neighbors know my name kinda love!

I want a it's okay to have girls' night out kinda love;

A this loving is so good I just gotta shout kinda love.

I want a when things are going wrong he rubs my back kinda love;

A we can sip wine you be my daddy mack kinda love!

I want a you paint my toenails I rub your feet kinda love;

A you kiss me every time we meet kinda love.

I want a you be for me, I be for you kinda love;

A I'll forever say I do, kinda love!

I want a stop on the side of the road and get it today kinda love;

A you be Barack I'll be Michelle role play kinda love.

I want a you can have whatever you like kinda love:

A for your love I will fight kinda love.

I want a one plus one equals one kinda love;

A we've only just begun kinda love.

I want a let's lay back on a lazy day kinda love;

A you be poker let's go and play kinda love.

I want a let's get married in the rain kinda love;

A nothing to lose everything to gain kinda love.

I want a drench ourselves under Niagara Falls kinda love;

A dance ourselves senseless at Masquerade balls kinda love.

I want a laugh until our sides hurt kinda love;

A you caress my thighs under my skirt kinda love.

I want a let's go to the movies and cuddle kinda love;

A when I write you write a non-rebuttal kinda love.

I want a teach me what I don't know kinda love;

A don't stagnate me, but let me grow kinda love.

I want a we outshine the sun kinda love;

A always remember to have fun kinda love.

I want a we have no regrets kinda love;

A there's no way we can forget kinda love.

I want a love that's open, free, and forever grows~

A love where intimacy, fire, and fun overflows!

I want love....

All I want is...that kinda love!

Chapter Seven

...HEAR ME ROAR!

Elisha McCardell

Historically Endowed

In my past life, I was a melanin strong woman trudging through the urine stained alleys in Harlem, screaming at the top of my lungs, "We know the road to freedom has always been stalked by death!"(Angela Davis). As my brothers and sisters crowd around me clothed in the darkest of blacks yelling, "Down with the genocidal tendencies of those in charge!!!" Even before that, I was a mother sweating large drops of blood pushing my way through the dense woods of Virginia seeking deliverance. Hardly bothered that the savior would come in the form of a rusted British ship lulling suspiciously in the harbor.

But yet, before that, I was a beautifully adorned queen.... Dancing rhythmically as the large beads of my ancestors crown my head as they shout in our native language... Swaying back and forth to the music of the Wagogo people in Tanzania...

J. M. Perkins

RARE

I am not just a woman.

I am remarkable.

I am more than a woman

I am an unforgettable women

I am that woman that is sketched in the minds

of many men because of my essence.

I am the one that he really wants but couldn't have.

I am that woman he compares to others and no one

comes close to the substance I possess.

I am an everlasting memory that never fades.

I am that woman that got away.

I am that woman that he couldn't live without.

So he found me, chose me and married me.

I don't want to be just a remarkable, unforgettable

woman.

I am a unique gem, a woman who fears the Lord

Shall be praised!

I am Rare as Rubies!

Jeslyn Lewis

Upon Becoming a Woman

The reality is that being a woman is not always about

sugar and spice and everything nice.

No...

Sometimes we have to be willing to pay the ultimate price.

With our bodies,

with our hearts,

and yes even our minds.

We sacrifice our love,

our space,

and our moments in time.

We know how to make a dollar,

when all we have is 15 cents;

We make good on our promises

and we mandate a consequence.

You see our issues run deeper

than the ocean's glorious blue;

And what you see ain't always what you get;

we know how to alter your view.

Some of us run in cliques,

while others stand alone;

It's not really about being every woman,

but about standing when all hope is gone.

The world expects perfection,

but I say just give them the real you;

Being a woman is about keeping it 100,

while making dreams come true.

We defy odds by

going beyond the call of duty;

We are made of strength that

people only see as beauty.

We add color to the rainbow and

 Sistah we speak to the storms;

We set the standard for living

by sometimes going against the norm.

Our positions may vary and

our titles range infinitely;

We find solutions to the problems;

we are more than enough definitely.

We specialize in smiling

no matter what's going wrong;

We demonstrate to the world

 how to sing our heart's song.

We RISE to the challenges

that would cause many to fold;

We have secret strategies

That are too great to be told!

We shhhine like diamonds and

are thus unbreakable;

We don't pause for danger

because we are unshakeable.

 We look well to our young

And we make our parents proud;

We speak with authority and

Sistah we move crowds.

We are go getters, and trailblazers,

We are trendsetters, and moneymakers;

We are head honchos, and top notchers,

We are originators, path shapers,

We are the beginning the beauty,

We are pillars of strength,

We are the depth and the height,

We are the width, and we are the length.

We march hard in combat boots

and step high in stilettos,

We promote quality of life and

look forward to tomorrows.

We are that sweet water that flows

 deep within the well;

We are that good love in the hearts of men that

 makes their egos swell.

We are that unforgettable element

 contrary to what others may think;

And when life serves us lemons

 we add OJ and vodka and enjoy a mixed drink.

We constitute the whole,

because we are not about fractions;

We may talk the talk,

but we definitely believe in action.

Now Sistah since you have now officially become a woman

You must know

that becoming a woman is far from an ordinary feat,

we are extraordinarily different, which exudes to every face we greet.

Sistah, I charge you to share this wisdom with the next sister who is…

becoming a woman.

Kimberly Monique Smith
Soul of Her Laugh

The Soul of her laugh exudes the strength no one has ever known other than herself. She chooses to keep it silent in fear of judgment of others. Yet it's the soothing essence that protects her from the inhibited happiness, which entangles within her.

The Soul of Her Laugh follows her to dimensions far beyond her natural comprehension yet guides her to a locality of satisfaction and jiggles her body like an intensive earthquake. Still the Soul of Her Laugh is her lifeline to grasp at the second of destruction.

She is revived by her soul and refreshed from her laugh, and the thought of this brings waves of invigorating jolt of tears resulting in shouts of charismatic pleasure of trembling no lover has ever been able to touch.

The Soul of Her Laugh symbolizes the freedom she has conquered from the darkness that once entangled her being.

Willetta J. Davis

OF A WOMAN

When they see me coming they all move aside

As I pass through

I see admiration and adoration in their eyes

I hear the wondering in their voices asking

Who am I?

Where did I come from?

Where have I been?

After my presence they ask

Have you seen her?

Will we see her again?

~

I have many names

I wear many faces

I've seen many things

I've been many places

I'm adorned in the Spirit

I am laced with dignity and pride

I'm as prayerful as Hannah

As graceful as Esther

As pure as Mary

In my heart is where truth lies

In my mouth there are words of wisdom

119

My tongue only speaks words of kindness

To my husband I am virtuous

My children rise and call me "Blessed"

~

I am respected and greeted by

Madame, Miss, Ms. and Mrs.

~

I am the Prince's Bride

I am Queen

Queen to my King

Queen of the land

I am Mother

Mother of Love

Mother of Nature

Mother of Abraham, Isaac, Jacob, Moses

and Jesus

I am God's greatest creation to bear great men

~

I am blessed with giving

My bosom carries the milk that nurtures many nations

My fingertips are numb from the grinding of the grains

These hands have prepared many meals and clothe many
who are naked

My womb carries the fruit where I bear daughters and sons

I'm exalted in the book of Ruth

Praised in Proverbs

And even Solomon has song me a Song

~

I am the sunshine on cloudy days

When it's hot, warm, or cold outside

I'm the months of

January, February, March, April and May

June, July, August, September, October, November and December

I'm always in your thoughts

Never forgotten

Always remembered

~

I am the Mother of the Civil Rights Movement

I am the Queen of Soul

I am the other half of man that make man whole

I am young

I am old

I am wise

I am bold

I'm always right

Never wrong

Or so I'm told

~

Many call me beautiful

Yet, I'm not vain

Though they adorn my feet with rose petals

It's to God I give the highest praise

I am highly favored

But, I'm not deceitful

Nikki says I'm Ego Trippin'

But, Maya says I'm Phenomenal

~

I am full of respect

Therefore, I am respectful

I will never be disrespected

Because I am respectable

Many have tried to belittle me

Beat me and break me

But I am...

UNBREAKABLE

~

I am far more precious than rubies

Far more valuable than diamonds, silver, or gold

I wear the finest of garments

Not of satin nor silk

But strength and honor are how I'm clothed

122

Men and children there is something that I want you to
know

When you are weak

I am strong

And...

when you slip

I am your backbone

~

I've been many places

I've seen many things

I wear many faces

And I have many names

Mother, Ma' Dear, Mama, Big Mama, Lil' Mama, Sweet,
Sweetie, Sister, Auntie, Baby, Girl, Honey, Chil', Lady, Pearl

~

I'm a strong, loving, caring, understanding one

I'm Black, White, Native American, Hispanic, Middle Eastern,
Indian, Asian, African...

~

I've been in this world since time began

Placed my mark in stone and sand

Became a mother to a motherless child

Taught the unlearned and nursed a sad heart into a smile

Sailed on the Nile

And...

I even slept in the Garden of Eden

For a little while

~

You see…

In the beginning God created an image of Him

and called him Man

And named him

Adam

And as he slept

I was created

Flesh of his flesh

Bones of his bones

And…

When Adam awakened

He took one look at me

Named me Eve

And called me…

~

"WOMAN"

Chapter Eight

Our HEro's Journey

Kimberly Monique Smith

Dawn of an Eye

He stands in the dawn of the morning in search of an eye of the sky.

As he walks, the dew of the grass echoes to the rhythm of his feet and roughness of his toes as he starts his journey in search of the Dawn of an Eye.

A Carousel swaying of trees led him into the quivering moment of an unfamiliar yet familiar feeling as he approached the edge of the dawn. The arrays of smell- of newness-expand his nostrils as wide as an open field. The beauty from the dazzling amazement flowing from the sun stretched his eye to the horizon once more in search of the Dawn of an Eye.

Finally, a shovel of morning dew lifted him to the anticipated arrival to the end of his journey. As he went beyond the circle of the morning, he realized it wasn't the Dawn of an Eye that he was searching for; it was He that was the Dawn of an Eye and the search was over. The peace of God had finally embodied him to a level of serenity only given to man from the Almighty Man. He was thankful his search was finally revealed. He bowed in humility to the creator of the Dawn.

Willetta J. Davis
African Warrior

great man of Africa
great African man
so strong and proud with dignity
he stands
 skin so deep
colored by the sun
as barbaric as Shaka
as mighty as Hannibal
harems of women adorn his feet
with great expectations
of becoming his Black Queen
with admiration
he sits proudly at his throne
as royal as King Tut
as powerful as Pharaoh
marks of battle embed in his skin
symbolizing protection
of his African land
guarding with his shield and sword
no savage creature
can defeat
the African Warrior

Jeslyn Lewis
KING SOULJAHS

Are you familiar with the story in the Bible about Aaron and Hur? If not, I encourage you to read about it in your spare time.

The Fallen Souljahs- Souljah with an H, but the H is often silent!
Inspired by: Jonathan Taylor

Look for the next few minutes,
I need your attention.
Today I'm going to be Aaron and I need for you to be Hur.
If you would listen for a moment, I believe you'll concur.
You see, we've allowed society to constantly belittle, take stabs at, and humiliate~
Our kings whose skin looks like ours!
Although vexed and often perplexed we can't afford to sit back and let them be devoured.
Our Kings need us to help them hold up the banner;
When the world tries to block and stop them, knock them down and shock them,
They need us to deliver that intangible manna-
Yes sistahs, we are to feed them, serve them, become beholding to them;
Because we have the hands that rock the cradle, but who really rules the nation?
Our men are dying of starvation. They are ravenous and our manna gives them
life!

That's how they conquer the strife... that society offers them daily
As Aaron I'll grab one arm and sistah, you grab the other;
Let's raise them up and fight with our brothas.
(Pause)

Though the bloodshed has been great, and it's not over yet~

When the enemy infiltrates our camps, we must stand strong with our vets...
The ones whose skins looks like yours and mine.
The ones whom we give birth to and love, let us rewind, give more time to refine and help them walk that line...
Because these are our fallen souljahs... that's S-O-U-L-J-A-H
But the H is silent~ it stands for HERO!
It's okay, I know you didn't know-
Our heroes are in need of hardhats because of the hardships that are hampered
upon them by haterz.
Thrust into in a hell that only our love can deliver them from-
The Hallowed ground they plow upon should be held in highest regard as a haven for those who harbor hope~
The help meets and Hurs who bless our King Souljahs with holistic harmony called honesty
See the H is not so silent when you really take the time to honor it.
As Aaron and Hur, let us start paying daily homage to our King Souljahs, our fathers, sons, brothas,
Our souljahs who have not fallen but have merely stumbled.

Our souljahs whose skin looks like yours and mine~
We can't erase time, but we can redefine the labels society has dishonored them with-
See niggas roll over and play dead!
King souljahs are leaders who lead by example and refuse to be misled.
Souljahs fight until the war is won'
They never give up or tuck their tails and run.
Real men recognize Aaron and Hur may sometimes be~
You and me
The Queen sistahs who reign.
King Souljahs love and provide for their children and give them their names.
And the shelters that house them for 9 long months-
Oh how they bless and honor them;
Never leaving them stranded or out on a limb

They stand tall and walk strong~
Disregarding how through the mud society tries to drag them
along.
The brown skinned men who deposit their seeds in our nesting
havens are vital to our reformation, revitalization, our royal nation;
So as society serves them up on platforms of degradation,
Let us grab one arm and then the other, for our King Souljahs are
comparable to no other brother!
The brown skinned babies born of brown skinned women, like you
and me
Heirs of the promise~

Redeemed, unleashed, and set free to reign as our King Souljahs
That's S-O-U-L-J-A-H, and the H is not silent it stands for Hero
Our heroes who rose from all the blows society throws as foes to
those
Who are brown skinned,
King Souljahs~ with an H which should never be silent,
But we all know that when we, as Sistah Queens humbly honor
them with holistic harmony and hem their garments with
wholesome honesty they rise up and take their place on hallowed
ground, no longer acknowledged as Fallen
Souljahs, but as King Souljahs who sometimes stumble but are
nonetheless, our Heroes!
Our King Souljahs, that's S-O-U-L-J-A-H and the H is NOT silent,
because it stands
for HERO!

Valencia V. Gibson
I Need That Kind of Hero

A Hero is a boy's dad who never leaves his side, one he can trust with every secret, allow him to cry, and then wipe the tears from his eyes.

One who will never miss a moment, not even when he sleeps.

A hero protects His family from harm, and the terrors by night that creep.

A Hero is a daughter's dream; the Husband she hopes to have.

One just like her papa who always makes her laugh.

The Hero she sees in the morning, thinks about at noon, and hugs at night.

One who dares not live without her, before he leaves her lonely, he would die.

He would never let her see him give up, he can't go a day without kissing her cheeks.

He'll cherish and never let her forget she is loved, no he'll never miss a beat!

A Hero is A Husband who stands through any storm, who would give anything for his family, while he seeks refuge in the Lords arms.

He teaches, and he cares about his choices, even the ones his wife makes... When there is trouble on the rise, he fights no matter what it takes.

Before he abandons his family, he will pray every moment past, and if he suspects he'll lose them even a little bit, the carpenter in him fixes it fast.

A Hero stands firm, and he cannot be moved, if he does not have everything he needs, he'll do whatever he has to do.

He makes a home for his family, he can't bear to see them in lack.

A true Hero although he may get tired, knows who to look too when he's lying flat on his back. Yes, I need a hero like that...

Kimberly Monique Smith
A Walk of a Man

You walked by me one day

I caught a glance of your walk that set my thoughts into a
wondrous twirl.

One step was rugged;

the other graced

reminding me of a boy striving to become a man.

A walk of an uncertain boy

wondering which way to escape the pressures of the moment.

As the days turned into months, and months into years

this uncertain boy's walk became of a seasoned man;

understanding the ways of his rugged journey.

His walk became calmer

because of the decisions he made to stay on the right path of life

instead of straying all over the place.

Slower from the troubles he did not avoid as a rugged boy,

and wiser because of the Grace given him.

This time when he walked by me

my glance was admired by the strength bestowed upon him

because of his journey he finally mastered.

J. M. Perkins

CROWN

His Spirit is drawn to her worth when he sees her because he recognizes himself in her-

He is the Source of vision and she is the resource of provision-

She is equipped and loaded with every fiber of his being-

As he writes the vision and makes it plain, His plans are germinated deep within the soil of her environment, cultivated and nurtured-

She captures his vision to help birth a nation filled with his hopes, dreams, wrapped up in his purpose-

It is through her that he is made whole and complete-

He is the house she builds with her hands and not tear down with her mouth-

His strength lies within her-

Granting her the ability and capacity to endure things that he was never created to bear-

He knows her voice when he hears it because before he saw her she spoke to him from within-

Wrapped in the compartment of her soul is a gift called "console"

Console the wounds of his broken spirit

Console him in his Lodabar place

Console him in the land of Nod

Console the little boy that lies under the beard and brands

Console tears of inadequacy

Console the shame that manifested itself into hurt, ache and pain

Console the feeble knees that wants to give up while on the road to purpose

Console the man that never wanted to be like his father but ended up him anyways

Console the boy in the man that had to be a man of his house at the age of 6

Console his broken heart of not knowing what love felt like from a mother

Console the ghost in his heart of wondering what it would have been like to know his father

Console the unworthiness of feeling like whatever he does it's just not enough

Console the looked over man that trains others for the position he is more than qualified for

Console the King in him that he has yet to sees;

We are here for you beautiful man of dust

Taken out of your side to be worn on your head, your strength lies between your ears-

Behold your helmet of protection- your "Crown of Glory."

Meet the Creatives of the Journey (Biographies)

Willetta J. Davis is a creative writer and spoken word artist. Creative writing has always been her passion. Her first love are children stories. She considers herself as a *Simple Inspirational Writer*. *"I write to inspire. I inspire to write. There is a (creative) writer in everyone."*

Over the years Willetta has focused most of her creative writing in poems, songs and spoken word. She published her first children's book, **Hi My Name Is C.J.**, and spoken word (poetry) **Of A Woman (written in the voice of the "Virtuous Woman")** in 2014. **Of A Woman** is her most cherished written work. "I believe in this piece because, I prayed and asked the Holy Spirit to tell me what He wanted me to say. And so, **Of A Woman** was created. Everyone has a divine purpose in life; I believe mine is to inspire. As a spoken word artist/poetess, I strive to inspire others to reach deep into themselves and unleash their inner poetic voice. Everyone has an inner voice that needs to be heard either to themselves or to the masses."

Willetta currently lives in Shreveport, Louisiana and continues to be creative. She believes that no matter what obstacles anyone is faced with and no matter how long it takes to reach their goals or dreams is to step out on faith and believe that you can do all things through Christ. "ALL THINGS are possible. Never give up on your dreams!"

Willetta Davis is a wife and mother of (Lucky) 7. She is a graduate of Minden High School (1990) in Minden, Louisiana and a proud graduate of Grambling State University (1995) in Grambling, Louisiana, where she received a B.A. Degree in Mass Communications.

Valencia Gibson is a published author of children's content and has collaborated with women nationwide in other books. She is a devoted wife, mother, and real estate entrepreneur. For as long as she can remember she has written the tales from her heart, and poetically expressed her feelings.

Jeslyn Lewis is... **~a Christian**... A work in Progress who serves on the Altar Ministry and the Serve Our Streets Ministry at Power Church International. Motto #1- WITH GOD, I CAN!!! **~ a mother**... A single mother doing the best she can for Paul, Patrick, Payton, Paydrea, Pavia and Talisa. She's the grandmother of 7 plus 1. Motto #2- Giving up is never an option; as long as you are breathing, you have another chance to get it right. **~ a daughter**... Hopelessly devoted to her parents Arthur Lewis and Dorothy Lewis **~ an artist**... Gifted to express emotions creatively. Jeslyn is the founder and CEO of *JesLovely Productions* and a published author of 2 books of poetry entitled, ***Portraits of Iridescence*** and ***Righting Wrongs by Writing Rights***. She has written, produced and directed 4 plays entitled, ***My Dreams Won't Let Me Sleep, I Wanna Know What Love Really Is, He Called Me Pretty*** and ***In R.A.I.N.*** (Real Adversity Is Necessary) ***We R.E.I.G.N.*** (Royally Elevated Igniting Grace Now). She also founded and for 6 consecutive years hosted a spoken word event called ***Words, Wine,***

Rhythm & Blues. ~ **a woman**... Still growing, still learning, but loving herself, flaws and all. Her journey to womanhood has been a rather tumultuous one, but she is EVERY WOMAN!!! She attended Grambling State University and the University of Louisiana @ Monroe matriculating in English. ~ **an advocate**... she fights tooth and nail for what she believes to be true. She is a 9-year survivor of domestic violence. She has been blessed to travel to Baton Rouge, New Orleans, Lafayette, and Lake Providence, Louisiana, Columbus, Ohio, and Mesa, Arizona to share her poems and personal story of survival from domestic violence and has testified at the Louisiana State Capitol for tougher domestic violence laws. Motto #3- I can't love you good, until I love me best! ~**a sister**... Working on relationships because she is her sister's keeper... ~**a friend**... Striving to be the very best bestie to the sistahs God allowed to cross her path. ~a peacemaker... If it ain't about peace, she wants NO PARTS of it! To be as good as she can, to all the people she can, in as many ways as she can, for as long as she can... that is the desire of Jeslyn Lewis. To become a philanthropist is her goal. ~**a lover**... So, in love with life, the joys and the pains because it takes both. ~**a part of God's plan**... When bad days come, she knows they won't last, so she trusts His divine will. She's... Imperfect, flawed, gifted, lifted, entitled, indebted, but still an heir~ She's only human... she falls short, she makes mistakes, but none that she's too anything to request forgiveness for.

She is a part of THE GREAT I AM!

Elisha McCardell is currently a principal at an elementary school in San Antonio, Texas. She writes in her spare time. She has self-published one novel, The Book of Sarah, and she has been a featured poet in, When You're Done Expecting. When she is not writing, she loves spending quality time with her four children.

Jont'e (J.M. Perkins) Perkins is the author of over ten (unpublished) books and devotionals. J. M. Perkins is a wife, mother, youth minister, motivational and self-development advocate, the author of a blog called, You-Volve, "Manifest the best version of yourself," and the editor and chief of digital magazine called, "I AM."

She has been in the field of healthcare for 20 years, but her love and passion has always been expressive communication through her writings, abstract poetry, photography and encouraging others to be the person that God has created them to be. She is an avid believer that your faith is pregnant with a promise which is your passion loaded with your gifts and talents. You are a gift wrapped up in greatness!

You can follow her blog at www.uvolve.info/

Kimberly Monique Smith is an Administrative Assistant with the City of Shreveport in the Shreveport Fire Maintenance division. She was born and raised in Princeton, La, on October 10, 1966. She is the oldest of five children of Lee Arthur and Gloria Jean Wiley Smith. Raised by her maternal grandmother, Beulah Turner Wiley, she was encouraged to write the events of her day because of her shyness, her gift of creativity and imagination was awakened. Kimberly began writing short stories, poetry at the age of 7 years of age. She wrote her first play at the age of 16, titled, Amelia's Christmas for her church. In 2014, she followed her dream of becoming a playwright she stepped out in faith and produced and directed her first play to the public, The Sisters Family. A play based on her mother and her two sisters and their family. In 2015 & 2017 she wrote and directed her next play, Amazing Grace. Recently she is working on a two-part play titled Before She Looked and When She Looked Up based on her own life.

Alisha Williams is a native of Shreveport, Louisiana. She loves writing! It's her passion! When writing, she wants to take you on a journey, evoke her reader's senses. She wrote her first poem at the age of twelve. She is a proud graduate of Southern University. While at Southern, she was a member of Phi Kappa Phi. She furthered her studies at Louisiana Tech and received a bachelor's degree in Psychology and was a member for of Phi Theta Kappa. In her work, you will find expressed views of the human psyche, as well as human behavior. Moreover, in her work you will quickly notice pieces filled with a host of emotions and imagery. She is a member of the Speak Entertainment, ArtistSwagg, Yahoo groups, The Poetry Corner and The Poetry Spot. "I love to network!" You can contact her on Facebook under Facebook under Alisha Williams or on her blog spot, www.poemotherapishoppe.wordpress.com

Begin your journey here...